Animals in my Backyard
COYOTES

Jordan McGill

www.av2books.com

AV² MEDIA ENHANCED BOOKS
ADDED VALUE • AUDIO VISUAL

Go to **www.av2books.com**, and enter this book's unique code.

BOOK CODE

Y22744

AV² by **Weigl** brings you media enhanced books that support active learning.

AV² provides enriched content that supplements and complements this book. Weigl's AV² books strive to create inspired learning and engage young minds in a total learning experience.

Your AV² Media Enhanced books come alive with...

Audio
Listen to sections of the book read aloud.

Video
Watch informative video clips.

Embedded Weblinks
Gain additional information for research.

Try This!
Complete activities and hands-on experiments.

Key Words
Study vocabulary, and complete a matching word activity.

Quizzes
Test your knowledge.

Slide Show
View images and captions, and prepare a presentation.

... and much, much more!

Published by AV² by Weigl
350 5th Avenue, 59th Floor New York, NY 10118
Website: www.av2books.com www.weigl.com

Library of Congress Cataloging-in-Publication Data

McGill, Jordan.
 Coyotes / Jordan McGill.
   p. cm. -- (Animals in my backyard)
 ISBN 978-1-61690-935-2 (hardcover : alk. paper) -- ISBN 978-1-61690-581-1 (online)
 1. Coyote--Juvenile literature. I. Title.
 QL737.C22M384 2012
 599.77'25--dc23
                          2011023414

Printed in the United States of America in North Mankato, Minnesota
1 2 3 4 5 6 7 8 9 0 15 14 13 12 11

062011
WEP030611

Project Coordinator: Jordan McGill Art Director: Terry Paulhus

Weigl acknowledges Getty Images as the primary image supplier for this title.

Animals in my Backyard
COYOTES

CONTENTS

Meet the coyote.

She looks much like a pet dog.

5

She lives with her family.

With her family,
she learns how to hunt.

6

She keeps warm with her fur.

With her fur, she is hard to see.

She talks with barks, growls, and howls.

With barks, growls, and howls, she can make 11 different sounds.

She hears with her long ears.

With her long ears, she knows when you are near.

She sees far and well with her eyes.

With her eyes, she can see the smallest animal.

She can run fast
with her strong legs.

With her strong legs,
she can jump.

16

She might live
close to your home.

Close to your home,
she finds things she needs.

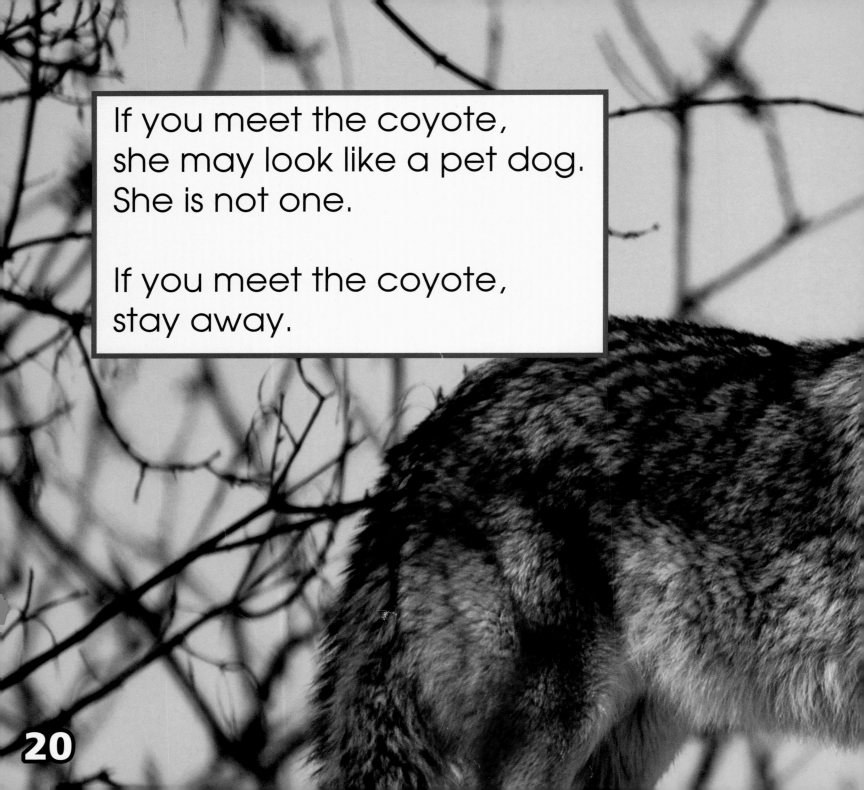

If you meet the coyote,
she may look like a pet dog.
She is not one.

If you meet the coyote,
stay away.

COYOTE FACTS

This page provides more detail about the interesting facts found in the book. Simply look for the corresponding page number to match the fact.

Pages 4-5

A coyote is about the size of a German shepherd dog and shares many of the same features. Coyotes are lighter than most dogs though. They weigh about 20 to 50 pounds (9 to 23 kilograms). The largest coyote ever found weighed more than 75 pounds (34 kg) and was 5 feet (1.5 meters) long.

Pages 6–7

Most coyotes live in packs. Most female coyotes have about three to seven pups at a time. When the pups are old enough, the parents teach the pups to hunt and live. At one year of age, the pups are full grown and ready to find their own packs. Some coyotes join their parents' pack.

Pages 8–9

A coyote's soft fur is gray, tan, or brown. Often, the fur on the coyote's back is black-tipped. The coyote's long fur helps to protect the animal from the cold. The fur turns dark in the summer and light in the winter. This allows coyotes to blend in with their surroundings.

Pages 10–11

Members of the dog family communicate and say how they feel by barking. They whimper, growl, and howl. They make these calls to defend territory and to talk with each other. A coyote's howl can be heard up to 3 miles (4.8 kilometers) away.

Pages 12–13

Coyotes have wide, pointed ears that stand up on the top of their head. They have excellent hearing. This helps them hunt and stay away from predators. Coyotes are omnivores. They eat meat and plants. Their main diet is made up of mice, small rabbits, birds, large insects, grasshoppers, and rodents.

Pages 14–15

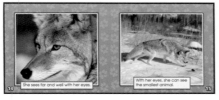

A coyote's sharp eyesight helps it find and catch prey. Coyotes have yellowish or green eyes with black pupils. They see moving objects best. Some small animals, such as rabbits, can escape coyotes by remaining still. Sometimes, coyotes will watch the sky for circling birds. Birds often circle in the sky above food.

Pages 16–17

A coyote's legs are strong and can move at speeds ranging from 25 to 43 miles (40 to 69 km) per hour. Coyotes cover about 2.5 miles (4 km) of land as they hunt each night. Coyotes can jump more than 13 feet (4 meters) high. That is more than twice the height of a van.

Pages 18–19

Coyotes are found throughout North America. They are remarkably adaptable. Unlike many other untamed animals, coyotes have increased their range since human civilization's rapid expansion. Coyotes once lived only in the deserts and prairies, but now they have come to inhabit much of North America. They can even be found in cities.

Pages 20–21

Coyotes are often found within city limits. Coyotes should not be approached. If a person encounters a coyote in nature, he or she should not run away. It is important to leave calmly and make loud noises to scare the coyote away. Never try to touch, feed, or tame a coyote.

WORD LIST

Research has shown that as much as 65 percent of all written material published in English is made up of 300 words. These 300 words cannot be taught using pictures or learned by sounding them out. They must be recognized by sight. This book contains 47 common sight words to help young readers improve their reading fluency and comprehension. This book also teaches young readers several important content words. These words are paired with pictures to aid in learning and improve understanding.

Page	Sight Words First Appearance
4	the
5	a, much, like, looks, she
6	family, her, how, learns, lives, to, with
8	keeps
9	hard, is, see
10	and, talks
11	can, different, make, sounds
12	hears, long
13	are, knows, near, when, you
14	eyes, far, well
15	animal
16	jump, run
18	home, live, might
19	finds, needs, things
20	away, if, may, not, one

Page	Content Words First Appearance
4	coyote
5	dog, pet
8	fur
10	barks, growls, howls
11	sounds
12	ears
14	eyes
16	legs